ELLIS ISLAND

ELLIS ISLAND
New Hope in a New Land

WILLIAM JAY JACOBS

Atheneum Books for Young Readers

To my father and mother, who chose
America, a land of hope and freedom . . .

Atheneum Books for Young Readers
An imprint of Simon & Schuster Children's Publishing
Division
1230 Avenue of the Americas
New York, New York 10020
Copyright © 1990 by William Jay Jacobs

Printed in Hong Kong
13 14 15 16 17 18 19 20

PICTURE CREDITS

American Museum of Immigration: pages 4, 9, 17, 19, 26, and
27; William Williams Collection, Research Collections of The
New York Public Library: pages 6, 10 (bottom), 11, and 12;
The Museum of the City of New York: page 18; the Byron
Collection of The Museum of the City of New York: page 3;
the Alfred Stieglitz Estate, page 5; The Library of Congress,
Map Division: page 16; The National Archives: page 20; The
Ellis Island Foundation: page 33; The New York *Daily News*:
page 21; Klaus Schnitzer: page 28; Ginger Chih, Peter Arnold:
page 30 (left); Dale Moyer: page 30 (right); Jeffrey Werner:
page 31; UPI/Bettmann Newsphotos: pages 13 and 22; Culver
Pictures: title page, facing page 1, and page 10 (top); Brown
Brothers: contents page; The Research Libraries of The New
York Public Library: page 14.

Library of Congress Cataloging-in-Publication Data
Jacobs, William Jay.
  Ellis Island / William Jay Jacobs. — 1st ed.   p.   cm.
Summary: Traces the history of Ellis Island and immigration
to America and describes the experiences of immigrants
arriving in 1907.
1. Ellis Island Immigration Station (New York, N.Y.)—
History—Juvenile literature.   2. United States—Emigration
and immigration—History—Juvenile literature.
[1. Ellis Island Immigration Station (New York, N.Y.)—
History.   2. United States—Emigration and Immigration—
History.]   I. Title.
JV6483.J33   1990   304.8'73'09041—dc20
89-38075   CIP   AC   ISBN 0-684-19171-7

Contents

1   *America! America!*   1

2   *Island of Hope and Fear*   7

3   *Opening the Gate*   15

4   *Closing the Gate*   23

5   *Remembering*   29

    INDEX   34

1

America! America!

March 27, 1907. A ship bringing newcomers to America steams slowly into New York Harbor.

People spill out onto the ship's deck. They push. They shove. They laugh. They point. They crane their necks for a still better look. Fathers lift their small children into the air so they can see the spectacular sight.

Looming before them stands the Statue of Liberty. In her hand she holds high the torch of freedom.

Some passengers burst into tears at the sight. Some freeze in complete silence, as if in prayer. Others sing happily in the language of their own country.

At last they are in America.

For three weeks they were wedged together in the steerage area, the ship's bottom deck. Sometimes during the journey the first-class passengers stood above and looked at them, amused. They tossed down coins or oranges or nuts. Then they laughed to see the poor people scrambling for the prizes.

Some in steerage brought their own

Sleeping quarters of steerage passengers, as depicted in an engraving from the London Daily Graphic *in 1870.*

food. For others there was nothing but black bread, boiled potatoes, watery soup. Many never left their bunks, even to go out onto their small deck.

The air inside was foul smelling. There were few toilets for the more than nine hundred people in steerage. Nobody had been able to take a bath. Many were seasick from the steady rolling of the ship.

In the excitement of arriving in America all of that is forgotten. In the busy harbor the passengers see great steamships and little tugs. Ferryboats crisscross between New York and New Jersey. Excursion boats carry happy crowds to the amusement park at Coney Island.

Rising in the distance is the skyline of New York City. Office buildings stand tall, like some jagged range of hills the travelers may remember from home.

To the left of their boat, near the Statue of Liberty, they see the redbrick buildings of Ellis Island. It is there, they know, that they will be taken. They will be examined by doctors. They will be questioned. And they will be told whether they can stay in America. Having

Passengers of the S.S. Pennland *on deck.*

Immigrants arriving on Ellis Island from a transfer barge.

come so far, there is the fear—almost terror—that they still may have to leave.

On this day, March 27, 1907, 16,050 newcomers arrive. It is the greatest number for any one day in America's history. Before the year is over, more than a million will pass through the doors of Ellis Island.

Most of them have left everything behind, even their families. Only a few know the English language. Strangers in a strange new land, they have no way of knowing what may lie ahead for them.

But they know what they want. Some want freedom to practice their own religion. Others are escaping from cruel governments. Nearly all have heard that in America there is a chance for jobs and for a better life.

And now they actually have arrived in "America, the Golden Land."

At the dock the newcomers leave the great steamship that carried them across the ocean. Then they are herded onto river barges for the ride to Ellis Island, where they will learn their fate.

Alfred Stieglitz's famous 1907 photograph, "The Steerage."

2

Island of Hope and Fear

In front of the castlelike main building of Ellis Island, guards quickly hustle the newcomers into line. Trudging beneath a large overhead canopy of heavy canvas, they enter a large hall.

Inside, they are greeted with a wave of sound. People speak in a babble of many languages, flailing their arms, shaking their fists. There is laughter, crying, screaming. Everywhere there is confusion.

The noise continues as they drop their bundles and baggage on the floor of the Baggage Room.

Then, once again, guards begin to shout and push them. This time they are prodded like cattle up a flight of steep stairs in twos and threes.

At the top they find themselves in the Great Hall of Ellis Island. It is a huge room, fifty-six feet high, with enormous arched windows. A large American flag is draped from a balcony overhead, and on the balcony stand a few well-dressed Americans. They look down on the newcomers with amusement, just as the first-class passengers did aboard ship.

Meanwhile, there is still more noise. More confusion. More pushing and shouting.

"Hurry up! Hurry up! This way!" demand the guards, leading them single file between rows of metal railings. At the end of each railing waits a doctor in the blue uniform of the United States Public Health Service.

The doctors watch as each group walks toward them. They look for people who may be blind or crippled. They look for signs of mental illness. Children older than two are made to walk on their own.

The doctors examine each person. Through an interpreter they ask questions. They want to know whether the newcomer is deaf. They want to see how alert he may be. They look for skin rashes, infections, hernias.

In their hands the doctors carry pieces of colored chalk. They mark letters on the coats of some newcomers: H for a heart problem, X for a possible mental defect, L for lameness.

An especially dreaded time is the eye examination. Doctors roll back people's eyelids with a small instrument. They are looking for a contagious eye disease called trachoma. Even if there is only a suspicion of eye disease, an E, for eyes, is marked on the front of a person's coat.

Those with chalk marks on their coats are separated from the others and put in wired-off areas called pens. There other doctors examine them. People with certain diseases are sent back to their homelands on the next boat. No one who has typhoid fever, smallpox, or leprosy may be admitted.

A child of eight or nine may be found to have a disease. When that happens the family must make a decision. Will everyone return with the child, or will just one adult go? It is a heartbreaking decision to have to make—and there is little time to think about it.

A child who is ten or older may be sent back alone, without an adult. But will such a child be able to make his way home alone from some port city in Europe?

An immigrant girl being given a psychological test as her family watches anxiously.

Newcomers undergoing phases of the physical examination.

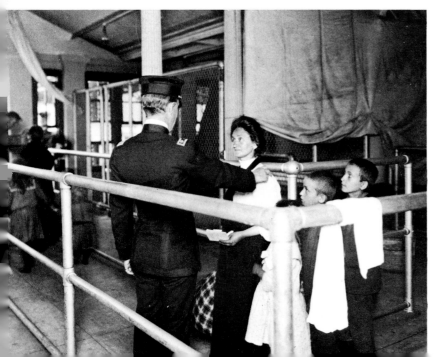

For those who pass the medical examination there is still one final test. Inspectors must ask each person a list of questions. Name? Married? Occupation? Ever been in prison? How will you earn a living in the United States? How much money do you have with you? Is anyone meeting you?

Most newcomers pass through Ellis Island in about four hours. About two out of every ten need more questioning or a longer medical exam. Only two of every one hundred are sent back home.

When they have passed inspection they go to the Money Exchange. There they trade the currency of their home country for American dollars.

Next those who are going to places outside of New York City go to the Railroad Room. After buying their railway tickets they are ferried over on river barges to railroad terminals in New York or New Jersey.

Those who will stay in New York City

A boy waits as his father exchanges money.

simply walk down a corridor to a door marked "Push. To New York." Often on the other side of the door they see happy relatives and friends waiting for them behind a wire screen.

There are tears of joy. Some of the newcomers kiss the ground of America. They give thanks to God. Men throw away their old peasant caps and black coats. Women put on new skirts that relatives have brought as gifts of welcome.

Then comes a short ride to Manhattan on the ferryboat. They marvel at the tall buildings. They stare open-mouthed at the automobiles.

In all the noise and confusion the busy inspectors have given some of the people new names. Sapirov has become Shapiro. Smalovsky has become Smith. Jacobovitz has become Jacobs.

That night, after three weeks on a ship, they will have baths. The next day they will look for jobs.

Immigrant families gather for a meal in the Ellis Island dining hall.

But now is the time to celebrate. The newcomers are becoming new people now—free people in a free land. They are becoming "Americans."

Happy immigrants take their first look at New York Harbor.

3
Opening the Gate

The story of America is the story of its newcomers.

In the beginning there was no Ellis Island. Indians simply walked across what then was a land bridge from Asia to Alaska. They were newcomers looking for better hunting grounds.

Christopher Columbus, a newcomer, was looking for something, too: a shorter trade route to India.

Still more people came. The Spanish conquistadors arrived, newcomers to a New World, searching for glory and gold.

More Spaniards came, including priests eager to spread the word of God. They settled in Florida and in what is today California and the American Southwest.

In 1620 the Pilgrims came to New England, and then the Puritans, looking for religious freedom.

Other men and women from England settled in Virginia and the Carolinas and Georgia.

The French came to Canada.

The Dutch came to New York.

The Dutch bought from the Indians a

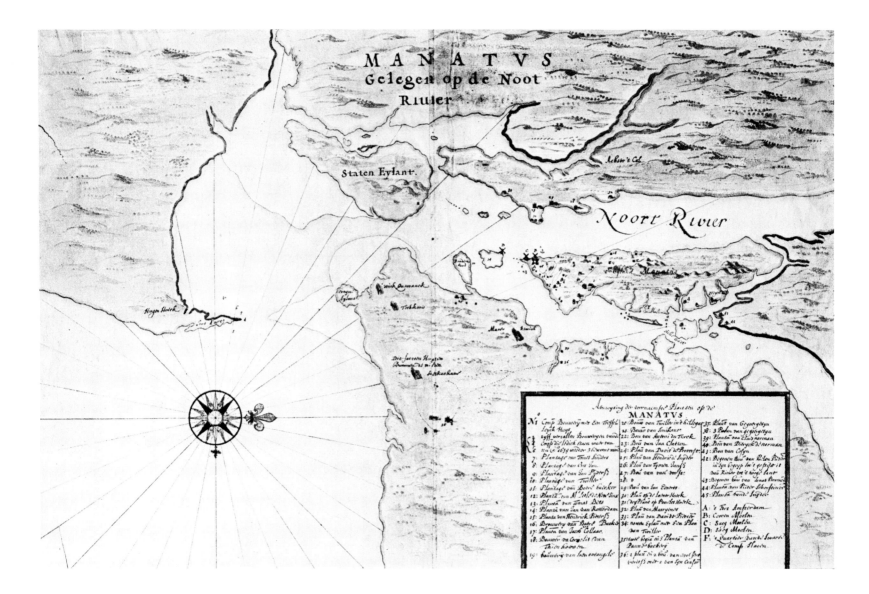

A survey map of Manhattan made in 1670, based on a Dutch map drawn in 1639 for the West India Company. This is probably the earliest extant view of Ellis Island.

tiny island near Manhattan Island. The Indians called the place Gull Island because only sea gulls lived there. But the Dutch noticed oyster beds everywhere and called it Oyster Island.

Later the British hanged pirates and traitors there on gibbets, so they called it Gibbet Island.

Just before the American Revolution, an American merchant, Samuel Ellis, bought the land from the British. He built a tavern on the island to serve the bay's fishermen. Now it was Ellis Island.

When Samuel Ellis died, New York State bought the island and sold it to the United States government. During the War of 1812 the government stored guns and explosives there. The United States Navy stored ammunition on the island during the Civil War.

Meanwhile, more and more newcomers were arriving in America. What started as a trickle grew into a flood.

Portuguese (top) and Spanish (bottom) immigrant children photographed in 1906 by Howard Giose.

They came from Ireland when the potato crop failed. Whole villages fled to America to escape starvation.

They came from Germany, looking for rich farmland in America's western states. Farmers came from Norway, Sweden, and Denmark, too.

Some people entered at Boston. Others came to Philadelphia or New Orleans or Galveston or San Francisco.

But most came to New York City. In 1855 the state of New York opened a station to receive them. It was called Castle Garden and was at the very tip of Manhattan Island. There the newcomers received medical care and could change their money into dollars. They were told how to travel to other places in the United States.

Still more newcomers arrived, in greater and greater numbers. But now they were from countries in southern and eastern Europe—from Italy and Greece, from the Austro-Hungarian Empire, and from Poland and Russia.

They were even poorer than the people

An early photograph of Castle Garden.

Immigrants photographed by Augustus Sherman, chief clerk at Ellis Island.

who had come earlier. They were fleeing savage treatment by their governments, and many had lost their land in Europe.

They were desperate. They had to be, to leave the only homes they had lived in all their lives and travel thousands of miles to a land where they had no friends and did not even know the language.

Soon Castle Garden was not big enough for all the newcomers who kept on arriving, so the United States government made Ellis Island the place of welcome for most of the people who came to America.

On Saturday, January 1, 1892, Ellis Island opened its doors. The buildings were not even finished. Yet 700 people were welcomed on that first day. In the first year 450,000 came, and by the end of five years over 1.5 million newcomers had arrived at Ellis Island.

In 1897 there was a terrible fire. The old wooden buildings on the island were all destroyed. No one was hurt, but the records of all the people who had come earlier were burned to ashes.

New buildings rose on the ruins of the old. The main building, with its Great Hall, was made of red brick and had towers that made it look like a castle.

Soon Ellis Island, too, grew crowded. Sometimes newcomers had to wait their turn for many days on ships in New York Harbor. In the year 1907 alone, more than a million newcomers arrived.

Generally they were poor and frightened, uncertain what life in America would be like.

From letters sent by relatives in America they knew that their jobs might be hard. They knew that greedy workers on Ellis Island might try to steal their baggage or cheat them at the Currency Exchange.

But newcomers kept on coming. They came by the millions, knowing that in America, in spite of all of its problems, they would at least have a chance. When it was their turn to write home, most of them said that in America they had found what they were looking for.

Workmen rebuilding at Ellis Island with fireproof materials after the fire of 1897.

A group of new arrivals in the 1920s.

4
Closing the Gate

In 1914 a great war broke out in Europe.

German submarines prowled the waters of the Atlantic Ocean, looking for enemy ships to sink. British warships waited outside German port cities, ready to pounce.

People were terrified to sail the seas, and newcomers no longer arrived at Ellis Island.

The Statue of Liberty still stood in New York Harbor, but there were few people to welcome.

When the war ended they began arriving again, but now there were new rules for getting into the United States. They were tougher than the old rules.

There was a reading test. People who came here had to show that they could read and write in some language.

There was a money test. Newcomers had to show the inspectors at least twenty-five dollars in some country's currency. That would prove they could take care of themselves. The American public would not have to take care of them.

A cartoon satirizing immigrant quota systems, from The Masses *(March 1913).*

Why were the rules so tough? Partly because American workers thought there weren't enough jobs to go around. Some of those workers once had been newcomers themselves. Now they wanted to keep other workers out of the United States.

After 1920 Congress passed even tougher rules. The rules set limits, called quotas, on how many people from each foreign country could come to America. It became very hard for people from southern and eastern Europe to get in. It was almost impossible for a person from Italy or Russia or Poland to start a new life in America.

Each year fewer and fewer people arrived. Before long, no newcomers set foot on Ellis Island. Instead, it was used as a prison. People were kept there who soon would be sent back to their home countries.

Then, in 1933, Ellis Island again began to welcome newcomers, most of them escaping from Adolf Hitler's brutal Nazis. Many of them, like the scientist Albert Einstein, became famous Americans.

During World War II Ellis Island was a station for the United States Coast Guard. Coast guardsmen trained there before going out to protect America's shores.

At the end of World War II many people with no home country to go to were allowed to come to the United States. They were welcomed at Ellis Island. Once again the buildings buzzed with activity.

But then, in the 1950s, Americans began to worry about newcomers, especially those who might be Communists. Congress passed new laws making it even harder to enter the country.

In 1954 Ellis Island was shut down. Only a few people were arriving, and it

An immigration service representative aids a newly arrived Dutch immigrant.

became too expensive to keep the buildings open. Except for a small crew of guards, the island was deserted.

The Great Hall, once crowded with people, was empty. Only occasional footsteps broke the silence.

The power was turned off. The buildings were cold and damp inside.

A once-busy ferryboat rested half sunk at the dock.

The buildings began to crumble. The roofs leaked. Plaster and tiles fell from the walls. Pigeons flew in and out through the broken windows.

The government tried to sell Ellis Island, but nobody cared to pay the price.

Ellis Island, the gateway to freedom and a new life, lay in ruins, nearly forgotten.

Facing page and right: *Ellis Island, abandoned, in the early 1980s.*

27

5
Remembering

In 1976 America celebrated its two hundredth birthday.

Birthdays are a time for looking ahead. They also are a time for remembering. In getting ready for their two hundredth birthday celebration, Americans once again began to remember Ellis Island.

Because visitors would be coming to the island in 1976, Congress voted money to help clean it up. Some of the visitors to the island became excited about rebuilding it.

It was decided to build a museum in the main building. Exhibits would help tell the story of the more than seventeen million Americans who had passed through Ellis Island from its opening in 1892 to its closing in 1954.

Today, newcomers no longer arrive at Ellis Island, but people still come to America in search of freedom. They come to escape from harsh governments like those of Cuba, the USSR, and the countries of eastern Europe. Some have survived the "killing fields" in the jungles of Cambodia and Vietnam.

An Asian girl and Hispanic boy are representative of the 1980s immigrants.

30

Some cross the border from Mexico to flee from troubles in El Salvador, Nicaragua, or Honduras. Some slip in on boats from Haiti.

Newcomers arrive from all over the world.

Once they are here they join together with the descendants of the Pilgrims and the Puritans.

They join with African-Americans, whose ancestors did not come through Ellis Island but came as slaves in chains to southern ports.

They join with Chinese-Americans, whose forefathers labored to build our railroads.

Today's newcomer, like every American old or new, has a story to tell about arriving in this New World. We are all wanderers or the children of wanderers. We are a people who have come to America fearing what might happen, yet hoping, somehow, for a better life.

Ellis Island, rebuilt, lives on as a reminder of that hope.

A young Israeli shows her "Green Card," which allows her to live and work in the United States.

Viewing the Statue of Liberty, an engraving from Leslie's Weekly, *July 2, 1887.*

THE IMMIGRANT WALL OF HONOR

The proposed new Immigrant Wall of Honor.

To honor family members who journeyed to America looking for "new hope in a new land," thousands of people have made contributions to help pay for the rebuilding of Ellis Island.

The name of each newcomer remembered in that way is listed on the Immigrant Wall of Honor at Ellis Island as one of the "courageous men and women who came to this country in search of personal freedom, economic opportunity, and a future of hope. . . ."

The wall is a tribute to the courage of those millions of newcomers who, leaving their homelands behind them, found a new homeland in America.

Index

African-Americans, 31
Austro-Hungarian, 18

Baggage Room, 7
Boston, 18
British, 17

California, 15
Cambodia, 29
Canada, 15
Carolinas, 15
Castle Garden, 18–19
Chinese-Americans, 31
Civil War, 17
Coast Guard, U.S., 25
Columbus, Christopher, 15
Conquistadors, 15
Cuba, 29

Denmark, 18
Doctors, 8
Dutch, 15–17

Einstein, Albert, 25
Ellis, Samuel, 17

Ferryboat, 13
Florida, 15
France, 15

Georgia, 15
Germany, 18
Gibbet Island, 17
Great Hall, 7, 21, 27
Greece, 18
Gull Island, 17

Haiti, 31
Hitler, Adolf, 25
Honduras, 31

Immigrant Wall of Honor, 33
Ireland, 18
Italy, 18, 24

Killing fields, 29

Land bridge, 15
Leprosy, 8

Manhattan Island, 17
Medical examination, 8–10
Mexico, 31
Money Exchange, 10
Money test, 23

Names, 13
New England, 15
New York, 13, 15, 17, 18
Nicaragua, 31
Norway, 18

Oyster Island, 17

Philadelphia, 18
Pilgrims, 15, 31
Poland, 18
Public Health Service, U.S., 8
Puritans, 15, 31

Quotas, 24

Railroad Room, 10
Reading test, 23
Revolutionary War, 17
Russia, 18, 24, 29

El Salvador, 31
Smallpox, 8
Southwest, 15
Spaniards, 15
Statue of Liberty, 1, 23
Sweden, 18

Trachoma, 8
Typhoid fever, 8

Vietnam, 29
Virginia, 15

War of 1812, 17
World War I, 23
World War II, 25